T0015820

SYBIL LUDINGTON'S
REVOLUTIONARY
WAR STORY

KATIE MARSICO
ILLUSTRATED BY THOMAS GIRARD

Lerner Publications ◆ Minneapolis

PUBLISHER'S NOTE

This story is based on historical events. The people, places, and dates are known through primary source accounts of the time. While inspired by known facts, dialogue and some descriptive details have been fictionalized.

To my daughters: Maria, Megan, Abby, and Lauren.
Like Sybil, you're all fearless game changers who
I know are destined to make a big difference!

Lerner Publications Company
A division of Lerner Publishing Group, Inc.
241 First Avenue North
Minneapolis, MN 55401 USA

For reading levels and more information, look up this title at www.lernerbooks.com.

The images in this book are used with the permission of: Architect of the Capitol, p. 30; Anthony22/Wikimedia Commons (CC BY-SA 3.0 US), p. 31 (statue); Wikimedia Commons (public domain), p. 31 (stamp).

Main body text set in Rotis Serif Std 55 Regular 15/24.
Typeface provided by Adobe Systems.

Library of Congress Cataloging-in-Publication Data

Names: Marsico, Katie, 1980- author.
Title: Sybil Ludington's Revolutionary War story / Katie Marsico.
Description: Minneapolis : Lerner Publications, [2018] | Series: Narrative
    nonfiction : Kids in war | Includes bibliographical references. |
    Audience: Grades K-3. | Audience: Ages 7-10.
Identifiers: LCCN 2017004827 (print) | LCCN 2017028711 (ebook) | ISBN
    9781512497854 (eb pdf) | ISBN 9781512456769 (library bound : alk. paper)
Subjects: LCSH: Ludington, Sybil, 1761–Juvenile literature. | Danbury
    (Conn.)–History–Burning by the British, 1777–Juvenile literature. |
    Women heroes–New York (State)–Biography–Juvenile literature. |
    Heroes–New York (State)–Biography–Juvenile literature. | United
    States–History–Revolution, 1775-1783–Women–Juvenile literature.
Classification: LCC E241.D2 (ebook) | LCC E241.D2 M67 2017 (print) | DDC
    973.3/33–dc23
LC record available at https://lccn.loc.gov/2017004827

Manufactured in the United States of America
2-50348-26761-3/5/2021

FOREWORD

Until 1776, Great Britain controlled the thirteen American colonies. Many colonists were angered by the heavy taxes they were forced to pay Britain's King George III. Those who opposed British authority were known as the Patriots. In 1776, Patriot leaders declared the colonies independent of British rule. Yet King George wouldn't let America go without a struggle. The fight between Britain and the Patriots was later called the Revolutionary War (1775–1783).

Colonel Henry Ludington commanded a local militia made up of four hundred Patriots in Dutchess County, New York. Most members of the militia were also farmers. In April 1777, Ludington's troops had temporarily set aside their weapons to plant their fields. It was a risk, but without crops, they would have little food that year.

APRIL 26, 1777,
SOUTHEASTERN NEW YORK

A cool rain stung Sybil Ludington's cheeks as she raced through the darkness. Her heart pounding, she clung to the reins of her horse, Star. Sybil was soaked, tired, and scared. Yet she was also determined to ride. That spring night, sixteen-year-old Sybil was on a perilous mission.

If the mission failed, her family—and countless others—stood to lose everything, including their lives. But Sybil didn't have a single second to waste on worry. Instead, she took a deep breath as Star charged through the open gates of a farm. It was Sybil's first stop that evening.

"Wake up! Wake up!" Sybil called out in a loud, clear voice. "The British are attacking Danbury! My father is Colonel Ludington. He needs you to spread the word and help gather his troops. When you're done, report to him as quickly as you can!"

A TERRIFYING TALE FROM DANBURY

Night had already fallen when word of the attack on Danbury had reached Sybil's home earlier that evening. Her seven younger brothers and sisters were asleep. Sybil was helping her mother with some sewing when frantic knocking shook their front door. Sybil's father opened the door to a messenger.

The man looked exhausted. Sweat dripped from his forehead, and his clothes were muddy from his ride. He struggled to catch his breath as he reported on events in Danbury.

Sybil's parents exchanged alarmed glances as the messenger's tale unfolded. The day before, roughly two thousand British soldiers had marched into Danbury, only 25 miles (40 km) from Sybil's home. The messenger described the deafening roar of their cannons.

"People were terrified, sir," he said. "Women and children were running through the streets. Most fled Danbury." The messenger paused and wiped his brow. "Not much reason for them to return now. The British set a good number of houses on fire."

"We must alert my men," said
Colonel Ludington. "Wake them.
Tell them to report to me here . . .
immediately! Come, there's not a
moment to lose!"

"It's no good, sir," the messenger told Sybil's father. "I'm sorry, but I'm afraid I'd fail you. I've been riding for hours, and my strength is gone. I'm not sure I could mount a horse, much less make the trip you're suggesting."

The messenger was right, but who could ride in his place? All their neighbors were miles away, and Colonel Ludington couldn't leave. If he did, there would be no one to organize the troops who managed to join him at his house. Sybil understood how desperate their situation was. And when her father turned toward her, she guessed exactly what he might ask her to do.

A DARK AND DANGEROUS RIDE

"Sybil, do you think you could sound the alarm?" Colonel Ludington took Sybil's hands in his. "It won't be easy, and there are many dangers."

Sybil didn't need her father to explain what those dangers were. She'd traveled country roads before. If she agreed to ride, she'd be cutting across soggy forests and fields. In many cases, her horse, Star, would have to race along narrow dirt pathways. Darkness would hide Sybil, but it would also hide any threats, such as wild animals and outlaws. And, of course, there was the possibility of coming face-to-face with British soldiers. What if the king's troops were already on their way to her town?

"Please, Sybil." Her father
interrupted her thoughts. "It is much
to ask, but you're our best hope." Sybil
didn't hesitate more than a second. The
ride would be a challenge, but she was
ready. Everyone and everything that
Sybil held dear depended on it.

So she kissed her mother good-bye. Then she hurried out to the stable with her father. As they put a saddle on Star, Sybil's father described the route she should travel.

Sybil's journey would take her 40 miles (64 km) through the New York countryside. She'd have to alert militiamen in towns such as Carmel, Mahopac, Kent Cliffs, and Farmers Mills. Then, if all went well, Sybil would ride home—where she hoped her father's troops would be gathered.

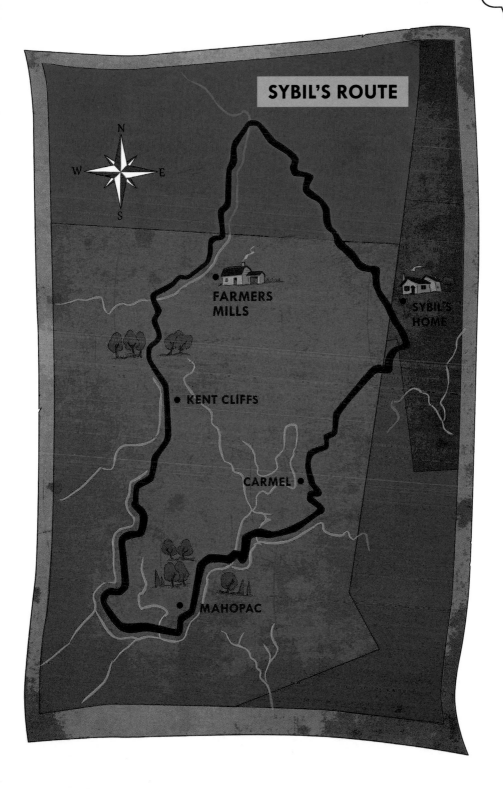

"I'll be back soon," Sybil whispered as Colonel Ludington helped her into the saddle. And with that, she and Star galloped into the pitch-black night. Before long, Sybil spotted the home of the first militiaman she had to visit and rapped on the shutters. As she delivered her news, the Patriot at the window put his hand to his mouth. Then the shutters slammed closed, and she found herself alone once more.

SOUNDING AN URGENT ALARM

Where had the owner of the house gone? Sybil drew her shawl around her shoulders. A chill crept over her. Suddenly she was seized by a new fear. What if the militiaman didn't believe her?

Sybil knocked on the shutters a second time. Just as she did, she heard the creak of a door. As Sybil turned toward the sound, she glimpsed a dark figure running toward her. It was the militiaman! He was still wearing his nightshirt, and the hat on his head was crooked. His coat was slung over one arm, and his musket was tucked under the other.

"Head on to the next town," the man told Sybil. "I'll round up the rest of the men that live in these parts. And mind yourself! Who knows where the enemy may be hiding?" Sybil nodded and guided Star back onto the road. She was one step closer to alerting the whole militia, but she still had a long night ahead of her.

As Sybil pressed forward, her mind wandered. Had any of her father's troops reported back to him yet? What was happening in Danbury? Where were the British troops? Sybil never let her thoughts drift too far, though. She needed to keep moving at a steady pace.

Suddenly, deep in the darkness ahead of Sybil, a branch snapped. She gasped and pulled on Star's reins. Luckily, it was just a fox prowling through the bushes. Sybil took a deep breath and rode on. She was determined to reach the other homes she still had to visit.

By the time she approached the final house on her route, her clothes were drenched. She and Star were covered with mud, and her hair fell across her forehead in wet, tangled locks. Her voice had begun to crack after hours of shouting the same alarming message. Yet, from atop Star, Sybil repeated it to one last Patriot. His wife handed her a cup of water. Sybil thanked her and eagerly gulped it down.

"So you're just like Paul Revere, eh?" the militiaman said with a chuckle. He rubbed his eyes and pulled on his boots. "Except that you had farther to travel." All at once, he grew serious. "Your courage may have saved us, girl. Get yourself home, and tell your father I won't be far behind!"

HEADING HOME

As Sybil neared home, the rain slowed.
The air was still. The only noises Sybil
noticed were the chirping of crickets
and the clop of Star's hooves. Once
the sun started to rise, she spied the
outline of her house. A thick fog hung
over the countryside.

"Please let our plan have worked," Sybil whispered to herself. She strained her eyes as Star trotted along the muddy path leading up to her home. Finally, the fog began to lift. As it cleared, Sybil saw the most welcome sight she could imagine. Hundreds of

Patriots filled her yard! Some were cleaning their weapons.

"Colonel Ludington!" a voice called out. "Sir, your daughter has returned!" Sybil's father bolted through the front door. Her mother and brothers and sisters hurried after him. They rushed past the militiamen toward Sybil and Star.

Her father helped her off the horse,
and her entire family embraced her.
As she searched their beaming faces,
no one said a word. No one needed to.
They were surrounded by proof that
Sybil's ride had been a success.

AFTERWORD

Because of Sybil's ride, local Patriots stopped the British from advancing much farther than Danbury. Eventually, famous Patriot leader—and future US president—George Washington personally thanked her for her heroism. The Revolutionary War ended in 1783 with the colonists winning their independence.

In 1784, Sybil married Edward Ogden and later had a son. She died in 1839. In 1975, the US Postal Service (USPS) created a stamp featuring Sybil's image. Statues of her also stand in several states. Sybil may not be as famous as Paul Revere. Yet her ride was just as valuable to US history.

TIMELINE

April 5, 1761 Sybil Ludington is born to Henry and Abigail Ludington in Dutchess County, New York.

April 19, 1775 The first shots of the Revolutionary War ring out.

July 4, 1776 Patriot leaders sign the Declaration of Independence, which declares the colonists free of British rule.

April 25, 1777 British troops attack Danbury, Connecticut.

April 26, 1777 Colonel Ludington learns of the attack on Danbury. Sybil begins her historic ride.

April 27, 1777

Sybil returns, having alerted most of her father's militia, who are gathered at her home. The Patriots force British soldiers in Connecticut into retreat.

September 3, 1783 The colonists sign a peace treaty with the British, effectively ending the Revolutionary War.

October 1784 Ludington marries Edward Ogden. They later have a son.

February 26, 1839 Ludington dies in Catskill, New York.

March 25, 1975

The USPS issues a stamp featuring Sybil Ludington's image.

LEARN MORE ABOUT SYBIL LUDINGTON'S RIDE

BOOKS

Abbott, E. F. *Sybil Ludington: Revolutionary War Rider.* New York: Feiwel and Friends, 2016. Read this work of historical fiction to find out more about Sybil's daring adventure.

Amstel, Marsha. *The Horse-Riding Adventure of Sybil Ludington, Revolutionary War Messenger.* Minneapolis: Graphic Universe, 2012. Check out this graphic novel for additional details related to Sybil's legendary ride.

Thompson, Ben. *The American Revolution.* New York: Little, Brown, 2017. Learn more about the American colonists' battle for independence.

WEBSITES

"Sybil Ludington (1761–1839)
https://www.nwhm.org/education-resources/biography/biographies/sibyl-ludington/
Visit this site for a closer look at Sybil and her impact on US history.

"Sybil Ludington, the Teen Patriot Who Outrode Paul Revere"
https://www.kidsdiscover.com/quick-reads/sybil-ludington-teen-patriot-outrode-paul-revere/
Head here for a summary of Sybil's ride, as well as links to sites and apps that deal with the Revolutionary War.

"Sybil's Story"
http://ludingtonsride.com/history.htm
Learn more about Sybil's life and how the Revolutionary War affected her family.